Online Privacy Survival Guide

Achieving Online Invisibility

for Asset and Reputation

Protection

By Naven Johnson

Contents

Introduction

The 21st century is not only an era of technical and computer innovations but the time when each of us can face a hackers' attack. You may have noticed that your computer started acting unusual, for example, suddenly opened a CD drive or launched programs without any command. Such a weirdness can be explained by system mistakes, but it's also likely to be outer intervention to your computer system. Of course, it's not a pleasant fact at all, and the majority of us will feel mad about someone breaking into our private space and playing with our property. Many Internet users become victims of hackers without even noticing it, but their attacks may lead to bad consequences including stealing your private information and crippling your gadgets. However, there's no need to panic! There are some simple tips and recommendations on how to save your digital space from perpetrators and where to go if something strange happens.

One of the basic signs that you were hacked is when you have a RAT (Remote Access Trojan). This program lets a hacker to get into your computer again and again without any suspicions from your side. A RAT allows remote users to connect to your system, providing full access to all the information, including your webcam. Sounds bad, but there is good news as well: it is possible to find out the hacker's IP address while he is connected to your computer. It means that if you notice someone else inside your system, it is possible to identify where the connected device is located geographically, and, moreover, to see login names and host names. This information will be quite useful for the authorities if you decide to address them. But, first of all, we need to understand how to notice that there is an attack on your device.

How can you be sure of being hacked?

We live in the times of regular cyber-attacks, and newspapers prove it to us daily, reporting of new precedents. Usually, they refer to serious crimes in which big companies and financial organizations are involved as victims. They lose data and money. But information about individual cases with common people is usually absent on their pages.

The thing is that the majority of people in the world have never thought of the hacking threat, and besides, they don't know how to find it out even if they have some surmises. The evolution of hackers' software has led to making them almost invisible and not easy to be discovered by a common user. Of course, nearly every modern device is equipped with antivirus or anti-malware software, which is usually quite effective. But if the defense was once weak for some reason and a hacker used his chance to get into the system, it's really hard to get rid of this infection. This happens because the contemporary malware is so sophisticated that it is able to fit into your computer system and pretend to be a part of important Windows system files that are never suspicious to most antivirus programs. Sometimes such malicious software replaces system files with no change of its functionality; they even save the original names. However, these newcomers add their own functionality that is not good for the system and especially for its user. Hence the system owner may have no idea of being attacked while a hacker gets a full remote access to the device and uses it on his own.

Why does somebody need your computer?

The main and the most popular reason why some hacker wants to get into your system is because it gives him a chance to steal a lot of your personal data, including access to the bank account and credit card. But, moreover, hackers are often interested in creating a thing called a "botnet." This net includes millions of infected devices all over the world that are ready to work with their commands. A botnet is under the control of a certain control center or a single user, and it is using system resources the way you can't do it. Some sources claim that about 40% of computers are connected to some botnet. The aims of such nets can be either harmless or lead to much more serious affairs. Luckily, there are several ways of detecting foes inside your system.

Preventative Measures

There is a great variety of special antivirus programs today, but it's important to be sure that the one you choose is capable of detecting viruses and malware such as worms, trojans, spyware, keyloggers, rootkits and other dangerous programs. Unfortunately, even the best antivirus examples can reveal a small percent of existing malware, about 10% maximum. Plus, every day new unknown virus programs appear on the web, and many of them were created with the ability to hide, change and improve themselves. So, the antivirus software is powerless facing many kinds of malware.

However, fitting up your computer with a fresh version of antivirus software is still considered a good defense from hackers. The AV specialists work hard to make their software better from day to day, offering new effective updates. Your software should be set on "active detection" mode in order to react to new suspicious occasions as quickly as possible and remove these intruders.

There's nothing wrong about feeling not confident in the IT related issues including AV software. The "Virus Bulletin" laboratory exists to make life simpler for everyone, as it specializes in evaluating the effectiveness of antivirus software. It makes its own objective conclusions on various programs and offers the results to be publicly available. So it's a great help while choosing an antivirus.

Preventative Checklist

Check Task Manager

When you have any thought that you may have been hacked, you are highly advised to refer to Windows Task Manager. You just have to push the Ctrl+Alt+Del combination and click the program name at the bottom of the new menu. You may also find Task Manager in your Start menu. When you click on the "Process" tab, a new window will appear. The thing we are looking for here is the CPU usage at the bottom. Notice the number: if it's higher than 10%, your system is safe, and there's no sign of attack. But if the percent is higher, your computer may be already infected.

System Integrity Checker for Windows

If you found out that something's wrong with your device, it's possible to get some more information about the attack.

Sometimes it may be possible to identify the other computer. Remember, that it is often hard to identify the attack because the enemy files pretend to be a part of the original system, and this ability hides it from the AV software. There is a special Windows tool called a system integrity checker (it goes under the name "sfc.exe") that may help, as it was created especially for helping users to scan the system for corruptions and restoring any corrupted files. This utility controls all the changes made in the system files and works on repairing them if it detects any damages. You can use it by choosing "Run as Administrator" at a command prompt (use right clicking). Then all you need to do is type the "sfc/scannow" command, then press Enter and see the results.

Netstat: Checking Network connections

All the malware that is intended to act against you is controlled by some hacker through remote access. It can't do you any harm without his commands through the net. Luckily, we can identify all the connections to your computer system with the help of another Windows tool, Netstat. You need to open a command prompt and type "netstat –ano" to find our whether your system has any unusual connections. This method works if the malware hasn't become a part of your system as was explained before. Unfortunately, some kinds of sophisticated malware are not visible for the Netstat.

WireShark

WireShark is another good tool for checking Network connections to your computer. This is an additional software that allows you to identify the dangerous and annoying malware connected to your system. The main advantage of WireShark is that it is an independent GUI-based utility and is it capable of revealing some malware that is invisible to the original Windows tools. It is also free and easy to download.

WireShark analyzes and shows the packets' flood that runs into your system, so if you know how the normal communication process of your system looks, you may notice some strange traffic and reveal the anomalous packets. In the case where you have no idea of how this process usually looks, you may look at your communications as a whole (using a special filter option). Hackers always try to avoid revelation using ports of high numbers. So you can try filtering ports from 1500 to 60000, and if there is any unwanted connection to your system, it is likely to show off. Besides, you may pay attention to traffic that is going out of your system, as the dangerous programs have to be connected to some external system and deliver information there.

If you want to create a filter in WireShark, type your command into the Filter window (it is located under the main menu). Type "ip.src ==192.168.1.103" (it's an example, so use your own IP address instead of "192.168.1.103". In results, you will get data on traffic coming out of your system. To filter it by port number you should type "and tcp.port > 1500 and tcp.port < 60000" where 1500 and 6000 stands for the range of involved ports. Then choose "Apply" to get all the data processed. So, after all, you get filtered information about your system's traffic that meets all your demands.

What should you do afterward is checking everything for strange traffic, different from a normal situation. It may require quite a lot of time and patience because you'll need to choose and type the IP addresses that you are connected to and don't know what they relate to into the browser and find if it belongs to a real legal website. If you find any strange or not working links, that's a reason to worry about. Considering all this, the installing and active using of antivirus software may be the most reasonable step to saving your system from hackers. After all, in spite of the imperfection, you may supplement your guarding programs with the tips mentioned above. Thus you may be sure if there is any unwelcome presence inside your computer system.

So, you are hacked. What should you do?

The situation isn't pleasant at all, and, moreover, it can be pretty dangerous for your computer and your private information. Good news: if you have already detected the attack, you are halfway to stopping it. Your primary goal is to understand what kind of malware you have to deal with. For example, if you were hacked with an application called TeamViewer, it is not a great problem to find out how to get rid of your "quests."

TeamViewer is used to get a complete remote access to someone's system. It sounds awful, but it is a real story. Hackers go through the following procedure to achieve this: logging into the machine, downloading and running an executable file, deleting the installer to cover the attack, logging off, and leaving a way to return to this system when they need to. Of course, when you spot some outer activity inside your property, it makes you super worried about the consequences. And that is pretty fair.

But instead of becoming paranoid it is better to start your detective journey right now and cope with the "enemy." The first stage is disconnecting your computer from the Internet until you finish your mission. It will help to be absolutely sure that now you are the only user of your device. The second stage is checking for any suspicious activity with the help of Activity Viewer of Task Manager. Ideally, you should know how your machine works and what the "normal" activities of the system are. For example, if you are familiar with normal level of memory usage is, and what kind of CPU usage is usual, then you can reveal strange working details through Task Manager and Activity Viewer.

The other thing you can try is tracking your network traffic. WireShark we've already spoken about is suitable here as the other programs that can monitor the network traffic which is getting into your system and leaving it. Consider monitoring your system after booting it up. Then it will be easier to look through several working applications and detect the strange ones if you know what the others stand for. Don't be confused by internet-connected applications that may run right after you switch on the computer or some other programs with the autorun mode. And, of course, if you have any problems with booting up your computer at your first command while usually, it reacts in a flash, it may happen because of someone else's current activity.

The next step is to do an inspection to understand what kind of harm the gatecrasher could do. The worst case is if their attack opened the full access to your machine. If so, it is impossible to predict what exactly they have already done, because they were not limited in their choice and could act like a typical user. So, what should you do now?

Don't Panic!

It may sound simple, but don't panic. The emotional reaction may turn the situation into something worse. You are not the only person on Earth to experience that, and this is not as critical as it may seem. Even if you are likely to lose some money because of the attack, it's not the worst thing in life to happen. Keep calm and start solving the problem.

Make sure you have disconnected from the Internet and checked your antivirus software. It must be up to date and ready to work. Open the program, switch on virus protection and start scanning the whole system. It is great if your computer is equipped with different types of anti-malware programs because the more, the better. Scan your device with all kinds of software that you have. It will improve your chances to succeed while detecting and neutralizing the malware.

Attentively investigate the results of scanning and remove all unnecessary and potentially dangerous files and applications. Unfortunately, even their deleting doesn't guarantee the full safety of the system. It's because there can be some malware installed in your browser that is able to continue its evil deeds. So be careful while looking through all the applications and test all the programs that you use. Remove all stuff that you consider strange.

Delete all your passwords and set new ones. This stage is extremely important when it comes to coping with a possible attack. But you can proceed to this step only when you are sure that no suspicious files are left in your system. Remember all the programs, websites, and applications you have passwords on, including bank and social accounts in the first place as they are filled with a lot of important personal information. If you can't be absolutely sure that your device is completely clean from all the malware, it is more reasonable to change all the passwords using any other computer that you can trust. And forget about using new passwords until the hacked computer becomes completely safe.

Clear all the history, cookies, cache and all the rest browser information. Besides, you need to log out of every account you have ever used. Social media sessions, email sessions, and all other sessions must be cleaned. We do this in order to stop any access to your profiles and information from this moment, even if someone had such an opportunity earlier. You may also consider signing up for two-factor authentication.

Be attentive checking out your email and social network activities. Look through all messages, including inbox, outbox, spam, and your address book as well. Double check of the system, in general, is even better.

All these steps are useful and productive, leading to neutralizing the attack and cleaning the computer. However, there is only one way to clear everything to 100%

safety. It is wiping the hard drive and reinstalling your operation system. Of course, it means that you'll lose all the data on this computer, but later you will have no reason to worry. Some specialists even advise to backup your system on a regular basis to keep your computer healthy and safe. You may have some important documents that can't be deleted anyway. If so, scan them with reliable antivirus and anti-malware software to be sure that they are not infected. In spite of the fact that individual folders are rarely damaged by malware, you should be aware that every file from the infected computer may contain dangerous stamps.

Don't forget to let your contact list know about you being hacked. They should be aware that they are in potential danger. Also, they may get some spam thanks from the attackers. Even if not so, it will be polite if you say that you have some problems with a connection to Internet at the moment.

Forewarned is Forearmed

There's no surprise that prevention is the best defense, and escaping hackers' attacks is not an exception. So, let's see what can you do to strengthen your protection.

A properly configured firewall will improve your defense, while the one with black points will make the risks higher, leaving ports open and hence making a computer visible for other Internet users. ShieldsUP! can help you with it. It is a website created for testing routers for any vulnerabilities. So you may scan your own router to be notified in case you have open ports.

An excellent antivirus software is likely to save your system. Your defense must be always on, while you should scan your computer on a regular basis. You may choose an original antivirus application that goes with your system or download another one. Avast Free Antivirus is often highly recommended.

Email may appear to be your Achilles' heel. Then be careful while checking your inbox and better not open suspicious messages. And, the most important, never open and download any strange attachments regardless of their type and title. It may be dangerous because an attacker may install malware through this file and you could never notice that there was any installation process. Remember that even the familiar address in the address box doesn't guarantee full safety, because the email of your friend or family member could be also hacked, so don't let your computer get infected. Looking for additional information about popular phishing scams and their prevention is pretty useful.

Security Holes

Avoid any so-called security holes. They procedure includes turning off Wi-Fi Protected Setup (WPS) on a router and disabling Universal Plug and Play (UPnP), what makes your device less vulnerable. Don't opt for weak, obvious passwords as they make the crime really easy for the hackers. Avoid opening suspicious websites. Update all the parts of your system as needed, and set notifications to do this if you tend to forget such things.

Your computer must be protected not only from the inside but from the outside as well; it's not less important at all. Never leave your laptop or any other devices unattended, even for a couple of minutes. A hacker doesn't need a lot of time to run a flash drive with malware or open some dangerous website through your browser. So be extremely careful while out of your house or office with a laptop.

Always switch it off when you don't plan to use it and make sure you have a proper complex password. Don't forget about the chance that your computer may be not only secretly infected by some malware but also simply stolen, so get used to doing a backup to a hard disc drive. In this case you at least won't lose the majority of your personal information that is important or memorable.

Do not share any secure information by chatting and messaging online. Hackers can easily attack your friend's page, ask for your personal info including bank details, for example, then hack your system or profile and proceed to someone next. Never give real answers until you are sure who the person on the other end is. Ideally, discuss this kind of information face to face if it is necessary and you really trust this person.

If you make sure that you were hacked, take control of the situation instead of panicking. Everybody feels angry, confused or frustrated when such a trouble happens in life, but try not to follow your worst emotions. Check all the barriers, look for any suspicious tracks and remove them, clean up the system and remember not to post any screenshots on the web.

Anti-Hackers' Lessons

The experience shows that the following tips do work for minimizing the thread. But don't forget that, unfortunately, even used together they don't provide full safety.

Passwords should be complex and different Each of us has dozens of accounts across the Internet, and the main advice here is to set different passwords for each profile. Choosing the same combination for several insecure pages increases your chances to be hacked exponentially. Be especially careful with social media pages and online banking. The second recommendation of primary importance is setting complex passwords that are longer than 10 characters. A password you can rely on must include both lower and upper case letters, and symbols and numbers as well. Never turn any personal information into your passport, because it may be known among other people or easy to find out. The random and illogical combination of symbols may be hard to remember, but it is worth choosing.

Antivirus and anti-malware should be always on
Make sure that your software programs are updated and ready to defend you from various malware. Latest versions are always the best. You can choose to download free software (AVG for example) or pay for other options (like Norton Antivirus). Downloading more than one antivirus application is a superb idea.

Username should differ from email address
It is common to choose the username similar to your email address, but it may be a fatal mistake. Better think of a name not easier than your password. The more complex and unrelated your username is the safer you are.

Safe URL for Facebook and email
It is not a well-known fact among the majority of users, but the difference between and "https://" and "http://" in URL lays not only in extra "s." The "https://" is way safer

than its shorter version. So set your settings on using this URL every time you log in.

Don't idle about updating your browser
If your Safari, Google, Internet Explorer or Firefox asks for downloading a new version, don't hesitate and let the browser get updated. The thing is that the new releases are often safer than the old ones and do a part of an antivirus's job. By the way, Google Chrome is regularly called the most secure browser of all.

Forget about public free Wi-Fi
Of course, it's a useful option for working outside your office and home, and we all love to find such a network access in a favorite café. But stealing your passwords through public Wi-Fi is super easy and allows attackers to act without almost any obstacles. All they need is to use a simple Firefox plugin. So think about the consequences before connecting to public networks.

Say no to sending important information

Sending private info over the Internet may cause many problems if your system is hacked. It's better to avoid swapping such messages using email or any chats. If someone gets access to your private account, they will get your secure data at their full disposal, so don't help them. Moreover, try not to save any secret information on the hard drive, as it is also vulnerable.

Make up tough security questions
A security question is an additional defense from hacker's attack, so take your time and think of a complex question and its answer complex enough. If there are only standard variants to choose from, like your first pet's name or a brother's birthday, the answer should be tough and made up rather than real. Then a hacker won't be able to change your password and shut down access from you.

Avoid using your PC Administrator account
The majority of people prefer using the Administrator account for downloading various software and applications. But non-

Administrator accounts minimize the chances of becoming a hackers' victim.

Back up regularly
Backing up everything you store on your hard drive to an external hard drive is not a paranoid idea. It's wise to copy all the needed information to some other device order to avoid accidentally losing it.

Get acquainted with phishing filter
Using fishing filter will help to prevent phishing scam. It will let you know if someone will make an attempt to attack your system.

If you are not sure of a link do not click on it
It refers mostly to your emails. Remember that official financial organizations such as banks don't practice sending crucial news by email. So if any suspicious message appears in your inbox, don't even think of clicking links inside. Instead of it better talk to your bank on the phone.

Pay attention to your account activity

Gmail account and accounts on the majority of social media include an option like "last account activity." Monitor it to always be aware if your account was used while you were away from your device.

Phone Hacking

While we spent more and more time surfing the net using our smartphones, hackers improve their skills and adapt them to new devices. So if you often use the Internet on your phone and noticed that it started acting in a strange way (for example, it switches on or off when is not supposed to, open apps and browser pages without your command, etc.), it's high time to consider a possibility of being hacked. Anyway, in spite the fact that all this may still happen because of usual system errors and bugs, it won't be too much to make sure.

First of all, track your phone activity for several days, especially at night. Does it follow only your orders or so something without your command? What pages and apps are run? What does it download and did any new programs and files appear on your device? Pay special attention to your mobile banking apps, credit services and shopping apps which you are logged in. You may notice that someone is spending your money at his own disposal without your permission and even knowing it.

If you answered "yes" to some or at least one of the questions mentioned above, it's likely to be an attack on your phone. Hence, the main task now is to realize how to make the "guests" leave your phone and close the door behind them forever.

The reason why phones are being hacked is usually financially based. Simply put, hackers want to steal your money. So you may start with a traditional procedure that everyone with infected phone usually follows, including canceling your credit cards, deleting suspicious apps, and so on. What you should never do, as you remember from previous paragraphs about computer hacking, is to act upon our feelings of anger, confusion, panic and others.

According to Chris Wysopal, the co-founder and chief technology officer of Veracode (a company which specializes in application security testing), you are at the highest risk to become a victim of phone hackers while downloading mobile apps. Yes, exactly these programs that seem to be harmless usually bring the worst damage with them. The Veracode reports say that there were more than 10 billion apps in 2010, and there is no single reason to suppose that their number have suddenly dropped in recent years. This number is huge and striking, but that is not all: the vast majority of these apps are not secure at all, and they never went through anything like a qualified security check. That's why each of the new apps you download to your dear phone make your risk to be hacked really high.

There was even a study at the State University of North Carolina. The Android Malware Genome, as the study was entitled, revealed that up to 85% of Android malware software gets into the phones with the help of repackaging. This hackers' technique means that they get access to your phone after you download an app. Previously, they go through a sophisticated procedure of downloading a popular app, decompiling it, and changing it by adding malware details.

Then they decompile the app and download it back to the market with a new name that differs a bit from the original one. Usually, users don't pay attention to such a small difference and download the application without any doubt, because they have no suspense that this game is original, legitimate absolutely safe. Of course, that is a crucial mistake. This malicious repackaging system often concerns mobile games apps as they are extremely popular among the audience.

To make sure that your smartphone is compromised, study its behavior. Every little strange detail can be a sign you are looking for. If you normally spend hours a day using your gadget and know everything about it, then you can surely tell how often it needs to be recharged. Notice if the battery acts as usually and doesn't require an extra "energy dose." If so, somebody may be using your phone with the help of remote access or the malware software may be running in the background. Professional know another way to detect an attack: they connect a device to a Wi-Fi network they can trust and see what kind of traffic the phone is sending. This tip helps to get to know if your gadget is delivering any information to some IP address abroad or something like that.

Besides, the least unpleasant sign that indicates a hackers' attack is if you start to get unreasonably long bills for calls and network traffic you are not familiar with. Hackers also work with premium text messages that you have to pay for and don't hesitate to make in-app purchases. You may think that they can't get rich with small thefts like that, but just imagine the profit when thousands of phone users are involved in this kind of affair. Hence, if something like this happens to you, it is most likely to be a real crime.

Thanks for Reading

Hello, this message is from Naven Johnson. I hope that you enjoyed this book and that it has helped your life in some way. It is my intention to create information that readers will find useful and valuable.

I am grateful when people read books and I are even more grateful when my readers leave a review. Please leave a review that lets me know what you liked about this book so that I can work on improving future books.

Check out a preview of another book from Naven Johnson

Irrational Behavioral Economics

Predicting the Unpredictable

By Naven Johnson

Do we always make rational choices? In other words: are all human's homo economicus? Certainly not. But this was not so obvious until the beginning of XX century, when the behavioral economics was developed. Behavioral Economics is a group of concepts which put into question the rational character of people's financial decisions.

Nowadays, behavioral economics concepts are used in many various fields:

Personal and public finances. "Save more tomorrow" is a program aiming at increasing pension savings among employees, by visualizing a future situation to the people. It is based on the Behavioral Economics findings: firstly, showing the reason of the situation: that people are too optimistic about their future (so therefore they save too little) and secondly by providing a tool to solve the problem: when confronted with a vision of the future people start being more realistic about their future.

Health. Campaigns towards giving up alcohol drinking are often based on Behavioral Economics concepts. For example, when an advertisement uses statistics comparing the amount of alcohol drank in different countries this changes the alcohol overuse issue from an individual to a common, society wide problem. In this situation, the following Behavioral Economics assumption was applied: social norms signal appropriate behavior in a situation of a whole community in danger.

Energy. Climate change: it is hard for people to perceive the long-term consequences of their actions, especially when the feedback to their everyday actions towards the goal is not visible. Feedback is needed. Based on this knowledge a solution was easy to find: a carbon footprint calculator was developed, showing how many trees you need to plant in order to absorb carbon dioxide emissions produced, day by day, action by action.

Thanks again!

You can find this book and others at most online retail sites.